Skull
Adult Coloring Books
Stress Relieving Patterns

7

John Daniel

Published by PUBLISHING COMPANY in 2016
First edition: First printing
Illustrations and design © 2016 Adult Coloring Book J. Kaiwell

allcoloringbook.com

All rights reserved. No part of this book may be reproduced or transmitted in any form or by any means, including but not limited to information storage and retrieval systems, electronic, mechanical, photocopy, recording, etc. without written permission from the copyright holder.
ISBN-13: 978-1539092322
ISBN-10: 1539092321

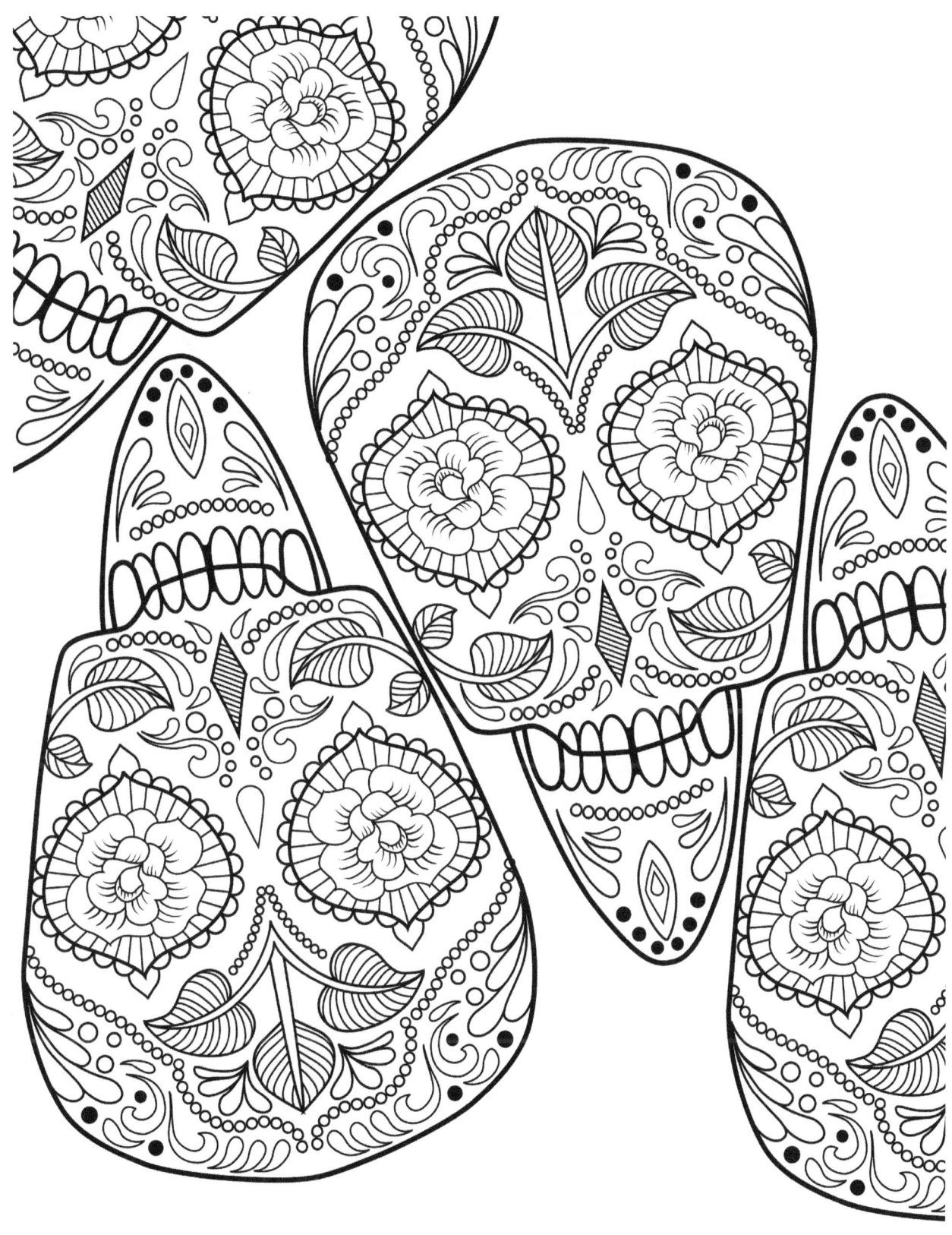

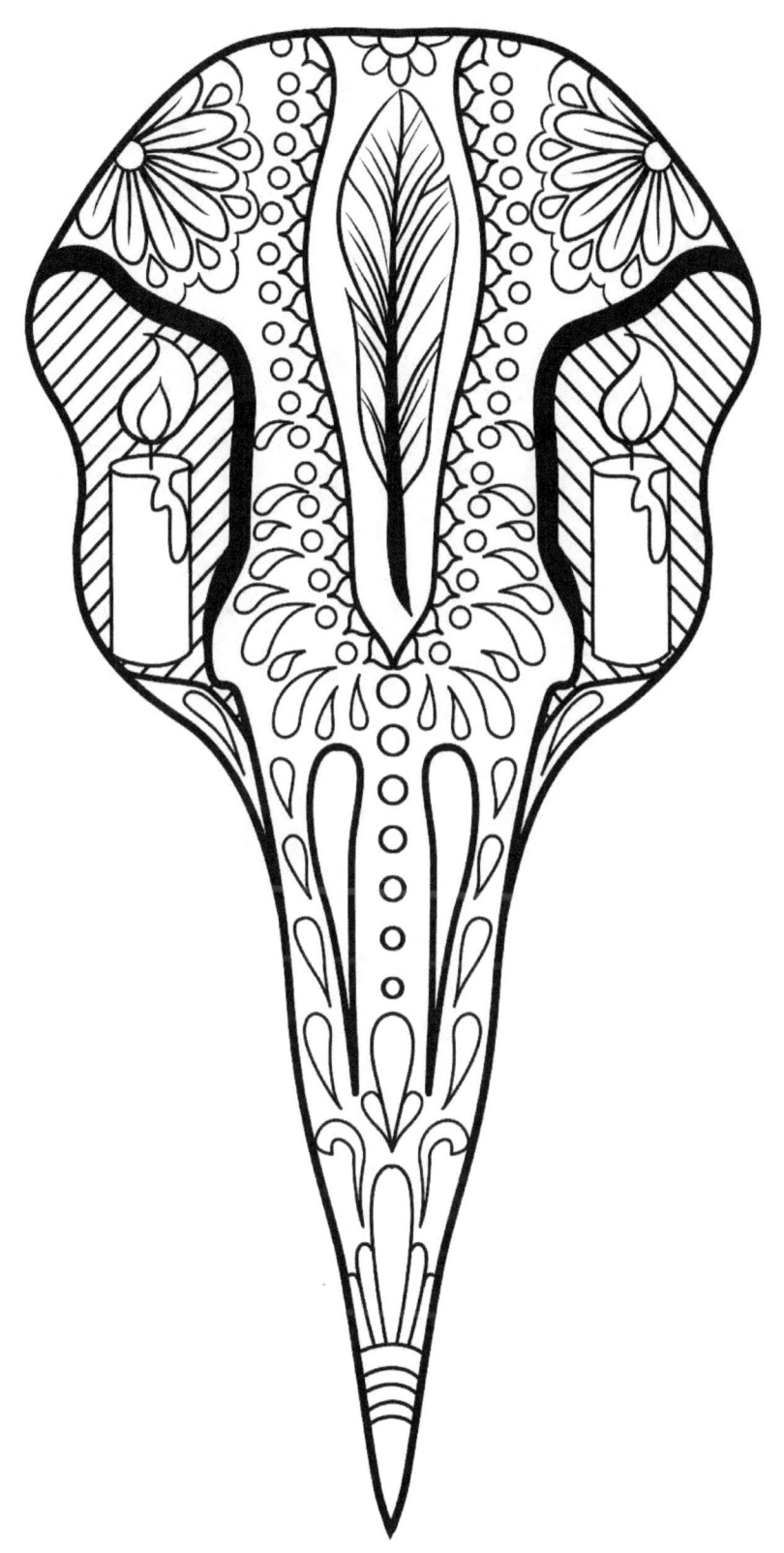

Thank You

Hope you've enjoyed your reading experience.

We here at Adult Coloring Book J. Kaiwell will always strive to deliver to you the highest quality guides.

So I'd like to thank you for supporting us and reading until the very end.

Before you go, would you mind leaving us a review on Amazon?

It will mean a lot to us and support us creating high quality guides for you in the future.

Thanks once again and here's where you can leave a review.

Warmly yours,
The Adult Coloring Book J. Kaiwell Team